Presented to:

_____

By:

_____

Funny, Deep, Wise
and Entertaining

My Comic
Quotes

Quotes designed to serve various purposes: to
boost your self-esteem and self-worth; to provide
the motivation necessary to chase your dreams; to
make you appreciate the simple joys of life, or to
simply put a smile on your face.

Emotional Intelligence Collection

Marcia Chorney

MY COMIC QUOTES

Copyright © 2021 by Marcia Chorney

First Edition: August 2021

ISBN-13: 978-1-7778431-8-2 (pbk.)

Publisher: Marcia Chorney

www.marciachorney.com

I dedicate this book to all my readers, hoping and wishing that the quotes and positive affirmations brought by this work will illuminate everyone's minds, bringing, therefore, a happier and more fulfilling life.

Cheers!

Marcia Chorney

L e t t e r s, uniting and forming, in this veritable tangle of words and thoughts that I carry in a gift box hidden in my head, where emotions and rationality meet and mix with memories of the past, the whys of the present and the dreams of the future; all together and mixed, in this tangle of unanswered questions, and the answers of many others.

This box of mine is a mixture of everything that creates and recreates: rules of life, father's advice, and mother's wisdom. A place where there are also the words and memories never forgotten of special people who passed in my life and then left; and of those who, before they left, placed their jewels of wisdom inside my box, which are there to this day.

So, I go on, day after day, accumulating these gifts in my little box; true precious stones, worth more than gold and silver; it is the wisdom of life, that is only found when much sought after. Most of the time the search is painful! It's sweaty! But once found, it becomes the producer of beautiful gifts, and the box will never be empty.

Marcia Chorney

Contents

Introduction

I always lived with this other girl inside me. In the beginning of our coexistence, we were very similar; in the middle, we were completely different; and now, I'm trying to look more like her, because she is exactly the way I always wanted to be.

She is another character, living, talking, thinking, and acting like she's an independent person inside of me.

She doesn't ask for permission to think and say whatever she wants.

She is fun, humorous, always in a good mood and always very positive.

She knows her weaknesses and uses them to her advantage.

She knows her limitations and accepts them well.

She calculates her actions and always makes decisions that will help her achieve her goals.

She is aware that her mind can be her best friend or her biggest enemy.

Speaking of friendship, she is an excellent friend, always willing to help when I need her. She loves to give advice and always has a word of knowledge to help me navigate the uncertainties of my life.

She is super analytical, analyzing everything that goes on around her, and, because of that, she keeps accumulating experiences and wisdom; consequently, her advice is extremely valuable.

She never thinks that what happens to her is in vain, not even the most insignificant thing. For her, everything has a reason.

Due to her characteristics, I learned a lot in life and grew as a person.

Her words brought me several answers that I had been looking for.

She is strong, determined, experienced, mature, intelligent, friendly and, above all, very bold.

She is the protagonist of the theater of life that takes place in my mind, and I now have the joy of sharing her with you.

I hope you love her as much as I do, but I also hope you benefit from her precious advice and, above all, that you have fun with her too!

Because of her joy and positivity, I began to love and value life like never before!

Are you curious to browse through her collection of quotes?

I hope so!

So, there you go!

Enjoy!

Marcia Chorney

SECTION ONE

My Comic Quotes

BY MARCIA CHORNEY

> "I DON'T BRING THE BAD THINGS FROM YESTERDAY TO TODAY. I START MY DAY AS IF NOTHING BAD HAS HAPPENED."

The secret to start my day lighter.

BECAUSE

I AM

BEAUTIFUL

THE WAY I AM!

I understand that my beauty is formed by a set of factors and not just my physical appearance. That's why I've already stopped trying to change myself!

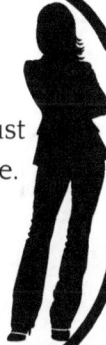

> **MAYBE NOT ALL MY PROJECTS WILL BE REWARDED, BUT I WILL PUT ALL MY EFFORT INTO EACH ONE OF THEM.**

I won't settle for less than the best!

> **THE BRIDGE IS CRACKED BUT NOT BROKEN.**
>
> **IT STILL SERVES TO LEAD PEOPLE FROM ONE BANK OF THE RIVER TO THE OTHER.**

I may be cracked but not broken, so I move on doing what I came here to do: **S H I N E!!!**

> I WON'T MISS THE
>
> OPPORTUNITIES OF THE
>
> # P R E S E N T
>
> BECAUSE OF THE
>
> GHOSTS OF THE
>
> # P A S T.

Didn't work before???

But now it will!!!

"

I AM INFLUENCING

PEOPLE

AROUND ME

ALL THE TIME,

FOR BETTER OR WORSE.

"

I will be more aware
of that!

> "
>
> ## I WILL NOT
>
> ## GO BACK
>
> ## TO WHERE I STRUGGLED
>
> ## SO HARD
>
> ## TO GET OUT.
>
> "

I will stay exactly
where I am!

> I MUST NOT WASTE
>
> ANY OTHER SECOND
>
> OF THIS
>
> SHORT LIFE
>
> WITH BITTERNESS.

"

I CONTROL THE THINGS
AND PEOPLE THAT COME
INTO MY LIFE SO I DON'T
HAVE TO DEAL WITH THE
CONSEQUENCES OF A
BAD CHOICE LATER.

"

Quality control **ON!!**

> I MAKE <u>MOST</u>
>
> OF MY DECISIONS
>
> # WITH MY MIND
>
> AND NOT
>
> # WITH MY HEART.

As they say, the
heart is deceitful...

" I STOPPED DOING

WRONG THINGS

WHEN I STARTED

DOING THE

RIGHT THINGS. "

How simple is this?

"HAPPINESS IS...

A WALK

ON THE BEACH

with the waves

touching my feet...

"

I will work hard to give myself this luxury every now and then.

I AM A V.I.P

VALUABLE

INCOMPARABLE

PRECIOUS

If I don't love and value myself, how do I expect others to do so??

"

MY WAY

OF LIVING

REFLECTS

MY STATE

OF MIND.

"

When I'm happy and at peace, everything gets clean and organized.

> I DON'T
>
> NEED TO BE
>
> **NORMAL;**
>
> I NEED TO BE
>
> # ME!

My normal is to be myself.

I CAN'T CHANGE ALL THE THINGS THAT GO ON IN MY LIFE, BUT I CAN DEFINITELY CHANGE THE WAY I REACT TO THEM.

> **I HAVE TO GET IT WRONG SEVERAL TIMES BEFORE GETTING IT RIGHT!**

"

HAPPINESS

IS FOUND

IN A

GOOD FRIEND!

"

Don't look any further!

19

> **WHOEVER**
>
> **HAS A**
>
> **GOOD FRIEND**
>
> **IS NEVER**
>
> **ALONE!**

My friend is just
a phone call away!

> WHEN I HURT A FRIEND,
>
> I PLACE A HEAVY METAL
>
> DOOR BETWEEN US.
>
> HOWEVER, I QUICKLY TRY TO
>
> REMOVE IT BEFORE THE DOOR
>
> GETS RUSTY AND STUCK.

" DRIVEN

BY

JOY!

"

I navigate life with a smile.

I WAS BORN

TO

SHINE!

That's why I left the shadows!

"

IF I TRUST MYSELF AND DO MY PART, I MUST NOT GET ANXIOUS ABOUT THE RESULTS.

"

No more worries, my dear!

> I ALWAYS LOOK AT A BAD SITUATION WITH ONE, TWO, THREE, A THOUSAND PERSPECTIVES IF NECESSARY. AS MANY AS IT TAKES FOR ME TO REACH MY PEACE.

It's my defense strategy!

I WON'T BE

THE REASON WHY

COMPANIES NEED

TO PUT INSTRUCTIONS

ON SHAMPOO!

I am a smart cookie,
and I will keep studying to
become a smarter cookie.

OMEGA!

"

IT'S OK WHEN SOMEONE

DOESN'T LIKE ME.

I DON'T LIKE

EVERYONE EITHER!

"

Hold your peace, babe!

> WHEN IT'S INEVITABLE
>
> TO DEAL WITH SOMEONE
>
> THAT I ABSOLUTELY
>
> CAN NOT SWALLOW...

HOLD YOUR PEACE A LITTLE LONGER, babe!

> # I LOOK
> # BETTER
> # WHEN
> # I AM
> # HAPPY!

My face doesn't look beautiful when I am angry, so if I want to always look good, I'd better always be **happy!**

> # THE PLEASURE
>
> ## IS NOT
>
> ## IN THE REWARD,
>
> ## BUT IN THE
>
> # ACHIEVEMENT.

When a dream comes true, no money can buy that feeling.

THE REWARD

IS JUST A

CONSEQUENCE

OF A GREAT

ACHIEVEMENT.

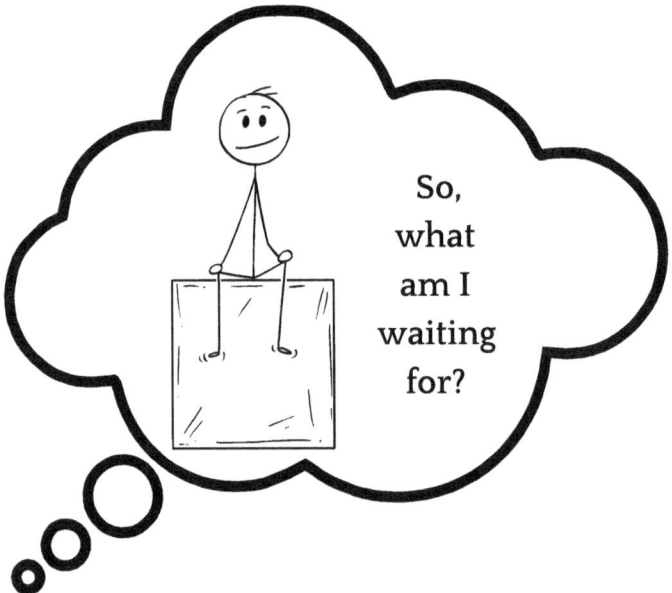

IN THE END,

I WILL FIND OUT

THAT EVERYTHING

WAS INSIDE OF ME

ALL ALONG.

So, what am I waiting for?

SECTION TWO

[My Comic Quotes]

BY MARCIA CHORNEY

> # " I WANT
>
> # TO GIVE
>
> # THE WORLD
>
> # MY BEST! "

"

I SACRIFICE MYSELF FOR A FRIEND WHEN NECESSARY.

"

It's so worth it!!

" HAPPINESS IS...

A

CUP

OF TEA. "

Occasionally, simply pausing my thoughts, sitting down, and savoring a cup of tea is sufficient to spark my joy.

I BEAT

MY ENEMIES

WITH

KINDNESS.

Because I will not
give them the slightest
chance to disturb my peace.

LOYALTY

IS A CROWN

THAT ADORNS

MY HEAD.

Without it,
I don't even
get out of bed.

TODAY

MY MIRROR

WAS

MOODY!

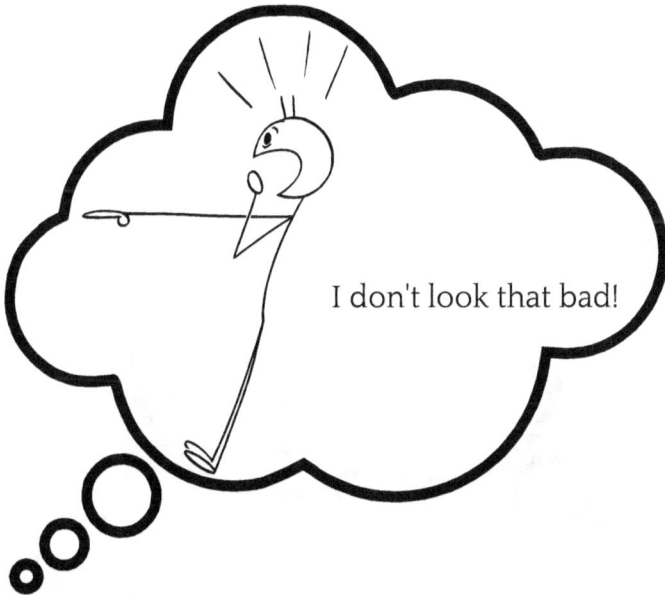

I don't look that bad!

I
HONOR
MY
WORD!

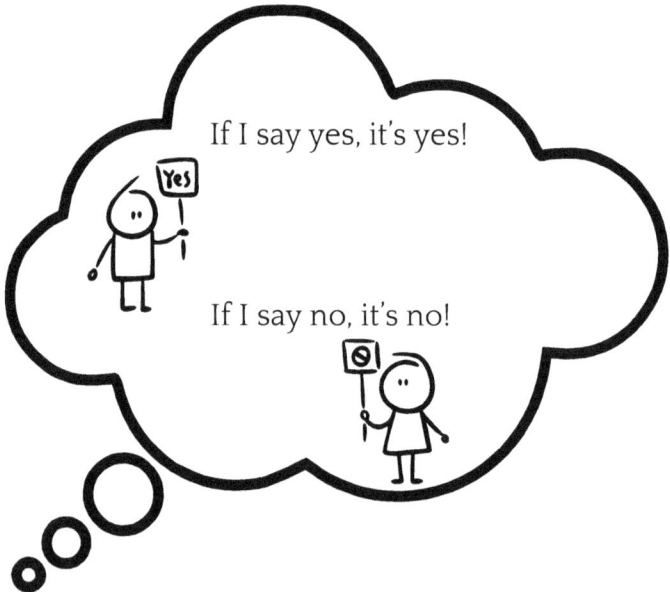

I GET

SO EXCITED

TALKING

TO YOU!!

That's why I interrupt you so much!!

> NOT
>
> ALL BAD
>
> HAS
>
> AN EVIL
>
> ROOT.

There is "good" bad.

IF I DON'T EVEN

UNDERSTAND MYSELF,

HOW SHOULD I EXPECT

OTHERS TO

UNDERSTAND ME?

Right???

I DON'T APOLOGIZE FOR BEING EMOTIONAL.

I let it all out!

ONLY

THE BRAVE

SHOW THEIR

EMOTIONS.

A coward hides them.

MY SECRET

TO LIVE IN SERENITY

IS TO TAKE ONE DAY

AT A TIME.

LITERALLY!

IT'S TIME TO STOP AND REFLECT ON THE THINGS THAT REALLY MATTER TO ME.

I'll take a break to think...

"

GIVING

AND

FORGIVING.

"

My best recipe for freedom.

I DECIDE

TO KEEP MY MIND

ONLY ON THE THINGS

THAT PUT A SMILE

ON MY FACE.

Why shouldn't I?

> **TO LIVE IN FEAR OF DEATH IS LIKE HAVING ALREADY DIED WITHOUT BEING BURIED.**

I don't worry; I just live!

> ## MY WORRIES DO NOT ADD ANY DAYS TO MY LIFE.

But surely, they take many away.

> **WHEN I DON'T**
>
> **HAVE THE ANSWER,**
>
> **I JUST DANCE!**

Shake that booty!

"

BAD YEARS

MAKE ME STRONG;

GOOD YEARS

MAKE ME HAPPY.

"

So, I go on living my life... Stronger and happier!

" THE TREASURE I HAD BEEN LOOKING FOR SO LONG WAS IN THE MOST UNEXPECTED PLACE. "

Those life surprises...

> # MY
> # PAST
> ## BECAME A SOURCE
> ## OF WISDOM FOR MY
> # FUTURE.

A guide to my current decisions.

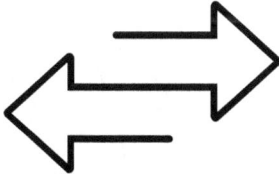

> **IF I DON'T CHASE MY DREAMS, THEY CERTAINLY WON'T CHASE ME!**

Run after them, my friend!!

SHOULD I CALL? OR SHOULD I NOT CALL?

Call this person. If they answer or return your call, they are a normal human being. But if they don't answer, it's best to stay away from them.

" LIFE HAS A CRUEL SENSE OF HUMOR. WHEN I REALLY WANT TO FIND SOMETHING, I CAN'T FIND IT. BUT WHEN I GIVE UP LOOKING, THEN I FIND IT. "

That's so annoying!
But it works!

> # I STAND FOR WHAT I BELIEVE!

How could I not?

" "

I AM THE LEAD ACTRESS

IN THIS GREAT ROMANCE

MOVIE PLAYING 24/7

IN MY MIND.

" "

Hopefully, someday,
somehow, I will leave
the screen...

> **WHOEVER**
>
> **LIVES**
>
> **WITHOUT**
>
> # HOPE
>
> **IS DEAD!**

Dream babe, it's free!

SECTION THREE

My Comic Quotes

BY MARCIA CHORNEY

" MY VIBE ATTRACTS MY TRIBE. "

I just have to be myself, and whoever identifies with me comes and stays.

> WITH TIME,
>
> EVERYTHING WILL
>
> START TO
>
> MAKE SENSE.

Just be patient,
my friend.

> **WHEN I DIDN'T,**
>
> **SOMEONE ELSE DID.**
>
> **IF I DON'T,**
>
> **SOMEONE ELSE WILL.**

Ideas must come off the paper.

"

SHOULD I STOP

AND GRAB

A PIECE OF

CHOCOLATE??

"

A constant question in my mind...

It's time to practice
self-control.

> **WHEN I LOWERED MY EXPECTATIONS OF PEOPLE, MY RELATIONSHIPS IMPROVED A LOT!**

Give people a break, sweetheart!

> **WHEN I REMOVED**
>
> **MY FOCUS FROM THE**
>
> **PROBLEM,**
>
> **THE SOLUTION**
>
> **SHOWED UP.**

Hey friend, it's time
to look to
another direction.

I AM SURE

I AM IN THE

RIGHT PLACE

AT THE

RIGHT TIME.

I have no doubt about it!

VISUAL COMMUNICATION SPEAKS LOUDER THAN ANY WORD.

Pay attention to your body language!

"
I WILL ONLY KNOW THAT

A PERSON IS NOT LOYAL

TO ME AFTER THEY

HAVE BETRAYED ME.
"

> ## TODAY
> ## IS THE DAY
> ## TO PAMPER
> ## MYSELF!

"

PEOPLE WHO WERE

DESTINED TO BE PART OF

MY LIFE HAVE ALWAYS

ARRIVED SURROUNDED

BY SIGNS TO CONFIRM

MY SUSPICIONS.

"

"

HOW

COULD I

LIVE

WITHOUT

JAZZ?

"

No way!!!!!!!!

"HAPPINESS IS...

A DISH OF MY

FAVORITE FOOD!

"

Yummy!!!!

But it tastes even better when
shared with someone I love.

HOW BAD DO YOU REALLY WANT IT?

So, fight for it, my friend!!

"
I WILL NOT HAVE

REGRETS

FOR THE

THINGS

I DIDN'T DO.
"

Because I am going
to do them!!

" WHEN THINGS GET
TIGHT, IT'S THE BEST
OPPORTUNITY TO GET
THE MOTIVATION
I NEED TO WIN. "

TODAY

I WILL

START

EXERCISING!

If I don't take care of my health, who will?

> # WHEN
>
> # I NEED
>
> # MOTIVATION,
>
> # I DANCE!

Just do it, babe!

"
I DON'T POLLUTE MY HEART WITH BITTERNESS AND ANGER.
"

As a way to preserve my health.

> **WHEN I LEFT MY COMFORT ZONE AND GAVE A CHANCE TO THE UNKNOWN, I DISCOVERED A WONDERFUL THING.**

Do not be afraid!
Take a deeper dive!

"

I

TAKE

GOOD CARE

OF

MY PETS.

"

It's a great way to practice
my kindness and I even
get love back! ♡

THERE ARE THINGS THAT I KNOW, THAT I KNOW, THAT I KNOW; THEY ARE MEANT TO BE MINE!

> **THE STONE
> THAT HURTS MY FOOT
> TODAY IS ALSO
> THE ONE THAT CAUSES
> MY HEALING.**

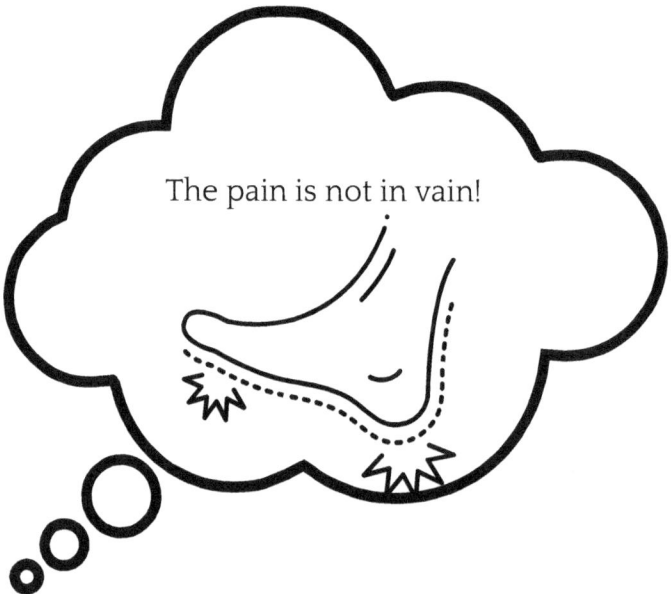

"

I AM GOING

TO TRY

A HAIRCUT

I'VE NEVER TRIED

BEFORE.

"

Sometimes, even I get tired
of seeing the same face
day after day.

> MUSIC
>
> TAKES ME
>
> TO PLACES
>
> I CAN'T GO...

Aww! Sooo good...

> **THIS**
>
> **TIME**
>
> **I GOT IT**
>
> **RIGHT!**

"

MY GREATEST GOAL

IS TO KEEP

LOVE, JOY, PEACE,

AND KINDNESS

IN MY HEART.

"

And I will achieve it,
no matter what!!!

" SELF-CONTROL

IS

SOMETHING THAT

SHOULD BE

PURSUED DAILY. "

It's a matter of practice.

SMART

PEOPLE

WEAR

PINK.

I love it!!
And I'm indifferent to people's baseless assumptions, even regarding the colors of my clothing. I totally feel like Elle Woods from "Legally Blonde."

IT'S

GOING

TO

HAPPEN!

Believe!!!!

THE FAMOUS CLICHÉ

'LIVE TODAY BECAUSE

TOMORROW DOESN'T

BELONG TO YOU', **IS THE**

PURE AND SIMPLE TRUTH!

Wisdom!

SECTION FOUR

My Comic Quotes

BY MARCIA CHORNEY

" I NEVER

MAKE DECISIONS

BASED ON

COINCIDENCES. "

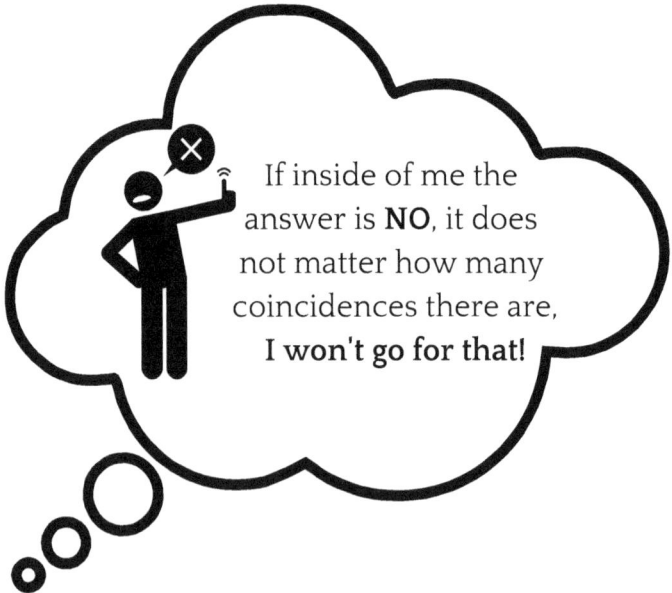

If inside of me the answer is **NO**, it does not matter how many coincidences there are, **I won't go for that!**

"

I WILL NEVER
GIVE UP
MY LIFE
AND
MY DREAMS.

"

Deep down I know that all this will pass... Everything passes, everything will always pass...

TAKE

AN

ATTITUDE!

Life is for those who have attitude.

I AM

JUST

FINE!

I have stopped looking for problems where there are none.

JUST BECAUSE

IT'S

FREE,

I DON'T HAVE

TO ACCEPT IT!

> IF THE SOIL
>
> IS DRY,
>
> THE PLANT
>
> DOES NOT GROW.

I water myself daily!

LOVE

MOTIVATES

ME!

I DON'T LIVE

IN THE PAST.

I AM NOT A

MUSEUM!!

I'm not there anymore;
I'm here!

" A GRATEFUL HEART

IS THE SECRET OF

HAPPINESS AND

SATISFACTION. "

I'm grateful for everything, even for the most "insignificant" things.

> ## WHEN I LOVE A SONG,
>
> ## I PLAY IT
>
> ## A THOUSAND TIMES
>
> ## IN A ROW.

My poor roommates...

But if that's what helps me get through a hard day, then so be it. I'm certain they would prefer to hear my music rather than my complaints.

> "
>
> I SURPRISE THOSE
>
> WHO DON'T
>
> LIKE ME WITH
>
> # KINDNESS.
>
> "

The reaction on their faces is priceless!

KEEP KICKING

THAT BALL

FORWARD,

BABE!

The goal is right ahead of you!

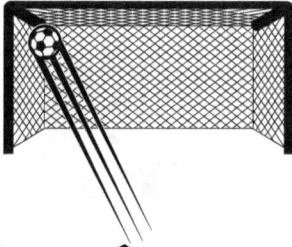

" I NEVER

ACT

WITHOUT

THINKING. "

Except in extreme situations,
which happens very often.

HAPPINESS IS...

MY PET!

My dog is worth more than that "bad dog" I was dating last year.

" WITHOUT LOVE YOU DO NOT LIVE, YOU JUST SURVIVE. "

Self-love; divine love and the love from those who genuinely care for you.

Remember that!

"
THERE IS NO EARLY

OR LATE, THERE IS

THE RIGHT TIME

FOR EVERYTHING.

"

Trust!

WHEN YOU HURT ME, I WILL LET YOU KNOW!

I won't leave anything stuck in my throat.

TODAY I JUST

WANT TO BE

THANKFUL

FOR EVERYTHING.

WHEN WHAT I WANT

IS NOT AVAILABLE,

I CHANGE MY MIND

AND FIND

SOMETHING ELSE.

I TAKE SUCCESSFUL PEOPLE AS AN EXAMPLE TO PERSEVERE WITH MY LIFE GOALS.

I always imagine them by my side saying: You can do it!

> IF YOU THINK OF
> YOURSELF LESS THAN
> EVERYONE BECAUSE
> OF YOUR SKIN COLOR,
> OR YOUR RACE...

Then you allowed racism
to get inside you.

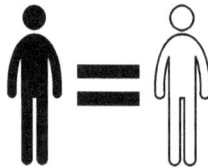

We are all equal!

> # I NEVER UNDERESTIMATE MYSELF!

The power is already within me; it just needs to be activated!

" I OVERCOME THE BARRIER OF MY FEELINGS. "

I do what I have to do, whether I feel like doing it or not.

"

I WILL ALWAYS

HAVE A

REASON TO

REJOICE!

"

There will be always
a reason to smile.

MISERABLE

ARE THOSE WHO

DON'T KNOW

HOW TO LOVE.

> # I LIVE IN A
> # MAGICAL WORLD
> ## THAT EXISTS
> ## WITHIN ME!

I forget what is outside!

" I DON'T

BELIEVE

EVERYTHING

I HEAR. "

I investigate further.

"

I WILL NOT

REPEAT

THE SAME

MISTAKES.

"

One fall is enough
to learn my lesson.

SADNESS IS A NORMAL AND FULLY ACCEPTABLE FEELING. WHAT IS NOT NORMAL IS MARRYING THIS FEELING FOREVER.

It must be a dance of push and pull.

" SOMETIMES WE HAVE TO TRY ONE, TWO, THREE DIFFERENT PROFESSIONS TO FIND THE RIGHT ONE. "

In the right profession, you won't feel that it is work, but pleasure.

SECTION FIVE

My Comic
Quotes

BY MARCIA CHORNEY

" ONE DAY I WILL REALIZE THAT EVERY BAD THING THAT HAPPENS IN MY LIFE IS TO TRANSFORM ME INTO AN AMAZING PERSON! "

And I know that I will be grateful for it!

> # I TAKE ADVANTAGE
>
> ## OF THE
>
> # SURVIVAL TOOLS
>
> ## I HAVE AVAILABLE
>
> ## TODAY.

I don't worry about the tools I'll need for tomorrow.

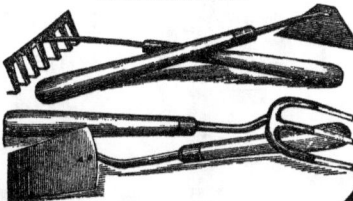

I AM COMING!!!

BROKEN, BLEEDING,

HURT, BUT

I'LL GET THERE!

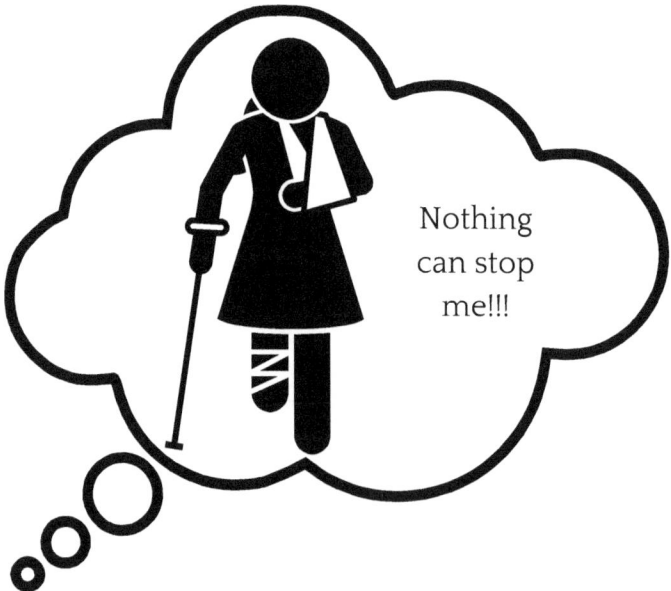

" I CAN WORK

SINGING AND

DANCING AT THE

SAME TIME. "

I'm pretty sure this isn't normal...

But who in this world is normal?

If you ain't a little crazy you ain't normal!

> **WHEN I LEARNED TO ASK OTHERS FOR THE THINGS I WANTED,**
>
> # RESPECTFULLY,
>
> **I GOT A LOT MORE.**

Lesson well learned!

"

FOR SOME PEOPLE,

NOTHING I DO WILL BE

ENOUGH FOR THEM

TO RECOGNIZE

MY WORTH.

"

I'll just forget about those troublesome people!!

SLOW PIANO NOTES

ARE LIKE A

SOOTHING REMEDY

FOR MY SOUL.

> TO ACHIEVE
>
> SOME THINGS,
>
> I MUST
>
> # SACRIFICE
>
> OTHER THINGS.

I won't fool myself. I can't have it all.

> **PAT YOURSELF ON THE BACK FOR ACHIEVING A GOAL, BUT NEVER PRAISE YOURSELF TO OTHERS. LET OTHERS PRAISE YOU.**

Your humbleness will make your work even more valuable.

" I WILL NEVER LOSE CONFIDENCE IN PEOPLE. "

There are still some who deserve my trust.

TODAY I'M GOING TO TAKE A RELAXING BATH, PREPARE A TASTY MEAL, PUT ON A NICE OUTFIT AND PLAY MY FAVOURITE SONG.

Just loving myself...

"

I HAVE THE

COURAGE

TO SPEAK WHAT I

FEEL TO WHOM

I LOVE.

"

To hide??
For what reason??
Fear of rejection??
Meh... I got over it!

" I WILL BE A

FAILURE

AS A PERSON IF I

CAN'T TALK ABOUT

MY FEELINGS. "

It doesn't matter how successful I am in other areas of my life.

"

TODAY I'M GOING TO TAKE A MOMENT TO SEE HOW A FRIEND IS DOING.

"

Cultivating my friendships...

HELLO!

"

COME ON

BABE!

YOU CAN

DO THIS!!!

"

Keep this positive vibe and go!!!

> # I
> # DESERVE
> # A
> # BREAK!

I will do it, and I won't feel guilty about it!

HAPPINESS IS...

A BOWL OF

ICE CREAM

ON A HOT

SUNNY DAY!

I'll do this too and
I won't feel guilty either!

As long as it's not every day...

" WHEN I LEARNED TO BE VULNERABLE, I BROKE DOWN THE WALLS THAT ISOLATED ME AND SEPARATED ME FROM THE PEOPLE I LOVE. "

Open your heart!

" I PREFER NOT TO PREJUDGE PEOPLE BEFORE GETTING TO KNOW THEM WELL. "

The times I did that,
I was always wrong.

"

EVERYTHING

FROM THE PAST

DECADES

ATTRACTS ME.

"

I often feel like an old soul adrift in the modern era.

> I VALUE
>
> EVERY
>
> **SMILE**
>
> I GET!

That's why I always give them back.

"

BETTER TO BE

REJECTED

FOR WHAT I AM,

THAN TO BE

LOVED

FOR WHAT I AM NOT.

"

I got to be authentic!
I got to be myself!
Whatever the cost!

> THERE IS NO LIFE
>
> WITHOUT CONFLICTS.
>
> **PEACE OF MIND**
>
> IS JUST A CHOICE IN
>
> THE MIDDLE OF THEM.

WHEN I AM REJECTED, I SAY: "OH POOR DUDE! HE WASN'T THE LUCKY ONE TO BE WITH AN AWESOME GAL LIKE ME!"

And good luck with your search!

THE WORLD

DOESN'T HATE YOU.

THIS IS ONLY

IN YOUR HEAD.

Fix that thought
right away!

"

THE WORLD WOULD

BE A MUCH BETTER

PLACE WITHOUT

CELLULITE.

"

And it would be even better
if no one was judged for having
them.
Freedom for my legs and butt!!!

Free my butt
from your
expectations!

> I CONSIDERED MYSELF A VERY COURAGEOUS WOMAN, UNTIL THE DAY I SPENT THE ENTIRE NIGHT AWAKE IN FEAR OF A LITTLE MOUSE THAT ENTERED MY APARTMENT.

"Are you a man or a mouse?" In this case... a mouse!

> MY LIFE IS A PERFECT COMBINATION OF NEGATIVE AND POSITIVE EXPERIENCES THAT ACT AS DRIVE SPRINGS, PROPELLING ME ON THE PATH OF SUCCESS.

That big push took me further!

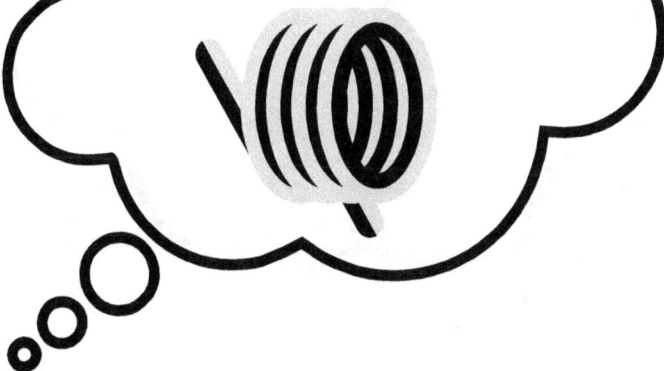

WHAT WAS ONCE

IMPOSSIBLE,

WITH TIME,

EFFORT, PATIENCE

AND PERSEVERANCE

BECAME POSSIBLE.

It was all up to me!

I ALWAYS FORGIVE MYSELF

FOR MY MISTAKES

OF THE PAST, SIMPLY

BECAUSE IN THE PAST

I DID NOT KNOW

THAT IT WAS A MISTAKE.

I take it easy on myself.

> **I DO MY BEST**
>
> **AND REST.**
>
> **TOMORROW**
>
> **I'LL DO IT AGAIN.**

One day at a time...

31

My Comic Quotes

BY MARCIA CHORNEY

SHOULD I

SEND

A MESSAGE?

OR NOT?

Send it, babe!
Take this anxiety out of your heart!

THINGS

WILL HAPPEN

AS THEY SHOULD

HAPPEN.

I will calm my heart.

> ## IF I WANT TO BE
> ## A WINNER,
> ## I MUST GET UP
> ## EARLY.

It is a MUST! Not an option.

> # I SET
>
> # MY GOALS
>
> # AND
>
> # MEET THEM!

I have discipline!

> A TRUE FRIEND IS THE ONE WHO SAYS, "DON'T JUMP OFF THE BRIDGE!" WHILE THE OTHERS JOIN THE CROWD OF SUPPORTERS: "I SUPPORT YOU, MY FRIEND, JUMP IT! JUST DO IT!

Is this your friend or enemy?

> THE FACT THAT YOU ENJOY
>
> YOUR OWN COMPANY
>
> SHOULD NOT HARDEN
>
> YOUR HEART TO THE PEOPLE
>
> WHO LOVE YOU
>
> AND ALSO WANT TO ENJOY
>
> YOUR COMPANY.

Open up to others!

"

IF I DO NOT GIVE

ATTENTION TO THE

ONE I LOVE,

SOMEONE ELSE

WILL GIVE IT.

"

Life is for those who act fast!

> **WHAT DICTATES MY HAPPINESS IS NOT WHAT'S HAPPENING OUTSIDE, BUT WHAT'S HAPPENING INSIDE.**

The inside is what matters.

" DRINK

WATER! "

This is one of the most important pieces of advice I can give you.

" NO INCONVENIENCE

THAT HAPPENS

DURING MY DAY

WILL BRING ME DOWN! "

> **IF IT DID NOT WORK WITH**
>
> **"A"**
>
> **THEN I WILL TRY WITH**
>
> **"B".**

That's the right attitude!!

> I
>
> BET
>
> I
>
> CAN!

> # THE
> # END
> ## OF ONE THING IS
> ## THE
> # BEGINNING
> # OF ANOTHER.

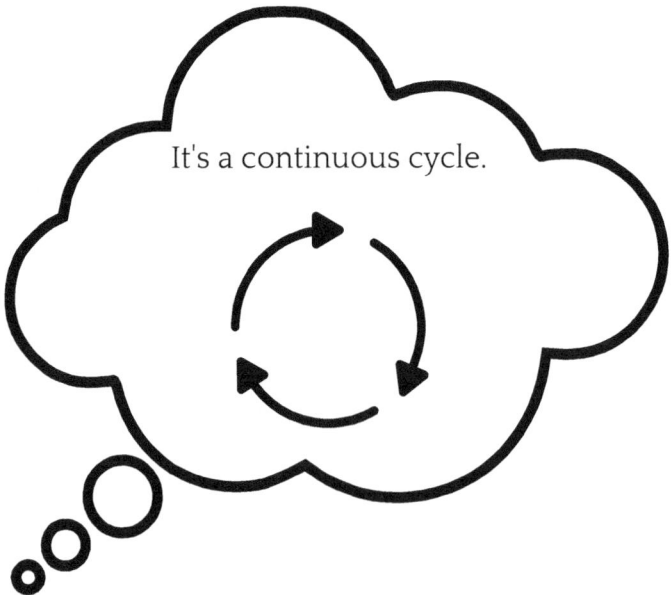

It's a continuous cycle.

> IF I STILL HAVE NOT FOUND WHAT I'M LOOKING FOR, THEN I WILL KEEP LOOKING.

That simple!

I GOT OUT OF THE ILLUSION OF "SHOULD HAVE BEEN THIS WAY AND NOT THAT WAY."

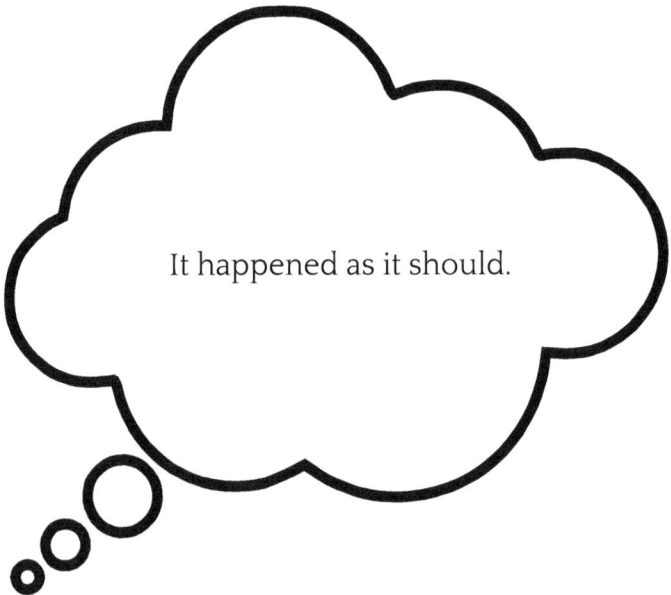

It happened as it should.

"IT HAS

TO BE MY WAY

OR ELSE I WILL

WHINE!!!"

BAD NEWS:
Childhood is over!
Time to grow up, baby!

> # I REST MY HEART KNOWING THAT WHAT IS MINE IS RESERVED FOR ME.

Not to worry...

> **BOOKS HAVE THE POWER TO MAKE ME FEEL THAT I HAVE COMPANY BY MY SIDE, EVEN WHEN I AM ALONE.**

A loyal companion
for all time!

"

I DO BELIEVE

THERE IS

A POT OF GOLD

AT THE END OF

THE RAINBOW.

"

There will always be something good at the end...

> # IF I DON'T FORGET
> # WHAT'S OUT THERE,
> # I WON'T GET
> # ANYWHERE!

> # THE INSPIRATION
> # I AM LOOKING
> # FOR IS ALREADY
> # WITHIN ME!

"

I USE ALL THE STONES THAT ARE THROWN AT ME TO BUILD MY CASTLE.

"

The more stones,
the bigger my castle will be.

"

BEAST

MODE

ON!!

"

ADVICE:

LOVE WILL MOTIVATE

YOU TO GO

FURTHER.

Trust me on this!

"

A SINCERE HEART

OPENS DOORS

NEVER OPENED

BEFORE.

"

> **THERE ARE PEOPLE THAT ENTER OUR LIVES BRINGING SUCH AN INCREDIBLE ENERGY THAT POWERFULLY LIFT US UP.**

Keep these people around!

> I AVOID
>
> WHAT
>
> IS NOT
>
> GOOD
>
> FOR ME.

Certainly. This is part of my self-care.

RELEASE THE TIES THAT HOLD YOU DOWN AND SHOW THE WORLD THE AMAZING PERSON YOU TRULY ARE!

Show your real self!

I PUT

A LITTLE BIT

OF HUMOR

IN MY DAY.

Every day!

I DO NOT EXPECT

OTHERS TO REACT

THE WAY I WOULD

REACT ON CERTAIN

OCCASIONS.

Everyone has the right
to be who they are!

My Comic Quotes

BY MARCIA CHORNEY

LOVE

&

RESPECT

"

I LISTEN TO THE

OPINION OF THE

ELDERLY,

ESPECIALLY

THOSE WHO LOVE ME.

"

They have my best
interest in mind.

LAUGHING

IS AN EXCELLENT

REMEDY

FOR ALMOST

EVERY ILL.

Overdose, in this case, is beneficial!

HAHA!

HAHA!

HAHA!

IF THE ODDS

ARE

IN MY

FAVOR...

"

I DREAM BIG

BUT

I SET REALISTIC

GOALS.

"

Avoiding disappointments
that can weigh me down.

> # WHAT
>
> # IS
>
> # PLANTED,
>
> # IS HARVESTED.

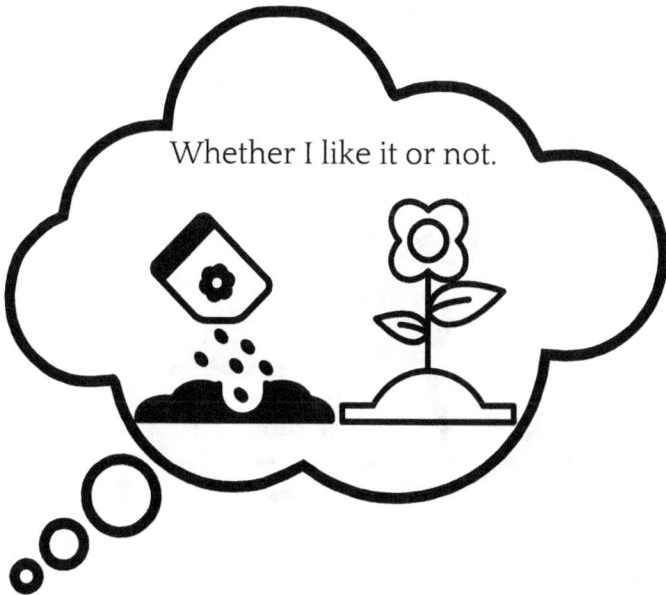

Whether I like it or not.

"
THOSE WHO ARE

SUPPOSED TO FILL A ROLE

IN MY LIFE, MAY DEPART,

BUT ONE DAY

WILL RETURN.
"

" I WILL NOT SETTLE

FOR LESS THAN

WHAT I

TRULY WANT. "

> **FOR EACH TEAR, A SMILE;**
>
> **FOR EACH MISTAKE,**
>
> **A VICTORY;**
>
> **FOR EVERY STUMBLE**
>
> **A RIGHT STEP.**

What I can't do is to stop my journey, lose faith, and give up hope...

A NOTE FROM

MY FUTURE SELF

TO

MY PRESENTE SELF:

"FORGIVE!!"

Forgive yourself and others. Don't waste more time!!

I STAY AWAY

FROM ANYTHING

THAT DISTURBS

MY MIND AND

MY HEART.

Absolutely!!

THE SECRET OF HEALTH IS KEEPING A JOYFUL HEART.

No matter the circumstances.

"

LISTEN

MORE

AND

SPEAK LESS.

"

I need to get better
on this one. I talk a lot!!!

"

I CAN SMELL

B.S.

KILOMETERS

AWAY.

"

It's a great skill to have!

> # I HAVE THE ABILITY
> # TO RESPOND TO
> # THE MOST OUTRAGEOUS
> # COMMENTS ABOUT
> # MY PERSON
> # WITH KINDNESS.

Because I am
a classy chick!

"

YOU MUST TRAIN YOUR
EMOTIONS LIKE YOU WOULD
TRAIN A PET DOG. PUT THE
COLLAR ON, HOLD THE LEASH
AND DISCIPLINE THEM
THE WAY YOU WANT.

"

> ❝ EARLY IN THE MORNING, IT IS POSSIBLE TO ENJOY A TYPE OF PEACE THAT YOU CAN'T ENJOY AT ANY OTHER TIME OF THE DAY. ❞

There is something about it...

" TAKE

A

DEEP

BREATH! "

As many as needed.

"

TAKE GOOD CARE OF

YOUR FRIENDS. YOU WILL

REALIZE THEIR VALUE

IN THE MOST DIFFICULT

MOMENTS OF YOUR LIFE.

"

HAPPINESS IS...

A

CHILD'S

LAUGH.

It is contagious!!!

> # SHINY
>
> # HAPPY
>
> # PEOPLE*
>
> ## I BELONG TO THIS TRIBE!

*R.E.M.

> **I KEEP THE GOOD**
>
> **TEACHINGS**
>
> **IN MY HEART**
>
> **AND**
>
> **I PRACTICE THEM.**

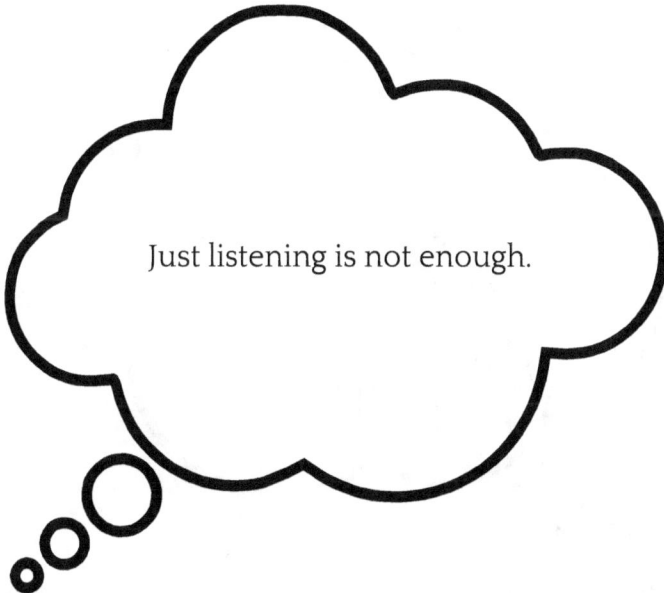

Just listening is not enough.

WISDOM

IS THE GREATEST

WEALTH

OF A PERSON.

I want to get
rich then!

> # I DON'T LEAVE FOR TOMORROW THE GOOD I CAN DO TODAY.

Tomorrow may not come...

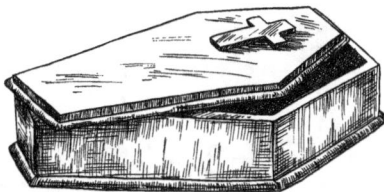

" THERE ARE WORDS THAT ARE SWEET AS HONEY, BUT IF YOU SWALLOW THEM, THEY WILL BECOME VERY BITTER. "

Learn to discern these words...

WHEN I MAKE

A MISTAKE,

I ACKNOWLEDGE IT,

I GO BACK AND

APOLOGIZE.

Doing that, I release
my own heart.

> # EVIL
>
> # DESTROYS
>
> # ITSELF.

I don't need to contribute to it. I'll keep my hands and conscience clear.

LIVE YOUR LIFE,

NOT

YOUR FEARS.

Don't be afraid, it's just **FEAR**!

False
Evidence
Appearing
Real.

HAPPINESS IS NOT LIKE A

COOKIE CUTTER.

EACH PERSON HAS A

DIFFERENT SHAPE FOR IT.

Find yours!

KEEP YOUR EYES ON

THE FINISH LINE

AND NOT ON

THE DIFFICULTY

OF THE MARATHON.

Keep going!

" MUSIC

IS

MY

MOTIVATOR! "

SECTION EIGHT

My Comic Quotes

BY MARCIA CHORNEY

> # FOR
>
> ## EVERY
>
> ## NEW DAY,
>
> # A NEW HOPE!

I expect good things!

> **LIFE CAN BE SWEET AS HONEY, WE JUST NEED TO BE THE BEE THAT PRODUCES THE HONEY.**

Hands-on, people!

" THOSE WHO

TRUST

THAT GOOD THINGS

HAPPEN,

RECEIVE IT! "

I must stay on this frequency.

> MY HAPPINESS
>
> DEPENDS ON:
>
> .
>
> .
>
> "ME"

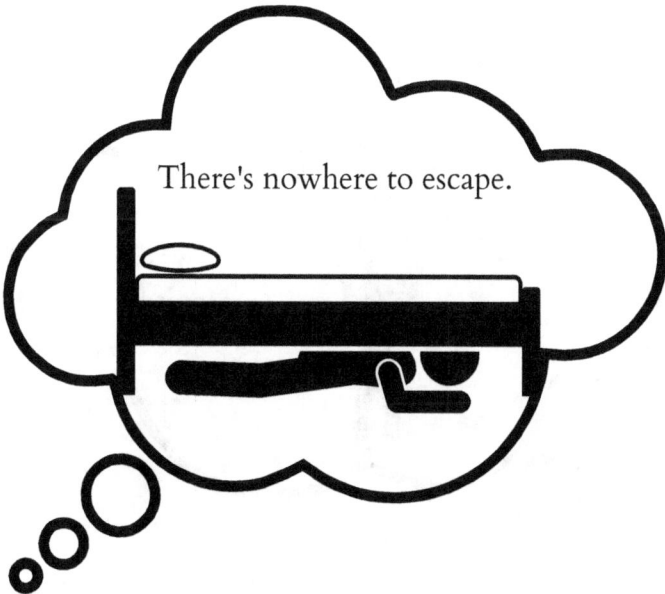

There's nowhere to escape.

"
I
LOVE
MY
BODY SHAPE!
"

I work my
way
around it.

"PLEASE"

"THANK YOU"

"SORRY"

MY FAVOURITE WORDS!

I use them many times a day.

"

YOU ALREADY HAVE ALL

THE TOOLS YOU NEED

FOR YOUR JOURNEY,

YOU JUST HAVEN'T

FOUND THEM YET.

"

With a more careful investigation, you will identify them.

I DON'T RUSH

INTO ANYTHING,

BECAUSE THERE IS A

TIME FOR EVERYTHING.

I finally understood that.

THERE ARE WISHES

THAT SCREAM

WITHIN ME.

BUT THEY CAN'T

ALWAYS BE SATISFIED.

I need to learn to live with this.

> THE SAME
>
> TRIED AND TRUE RECIPE
>
> WILL NOT ALWAYS
>
> COME OUT WELL.
>
> SOMETIMES THERE IS
>
> A PROBLEM WITH ONE
>
> OF THE INGREDIENTS.

Identify it, replace it
and try again.

Recipe

I NEED MY MORNING KICK, EVERY MORNING!

Go get yours, whatever it is!

"

I FINALLY LEARNED

TO BE HAPPY

AND SATISFIED

WITH WHAT I

HAVE TODAY!

"

I will no longer wait for
tomorrow to be happy!

"

I WILL USE MY LIFE

TO DO SOMETHING

POSITIVE

FOR THE WORLD

WHILE I AM IN IT.

"

The smallest gesture will make a big difference.

MIRACLES

HAPPEN

EVERY DAY.

Pay more attention around you.

"

WHEN

CONTEMPLATING

LIFE,

DON'T FORGET

THE SMALL DETAILS.

"

There is a lot
of beauty in small
things.

> **YOU ARE THE ONLY PERSON IN THE WORLD WHO PERFECTLY UNDERSTANDS THE INNER STRUGGLES YOU FACE.**

But you don't have to face them alone.

"HEY, I LOVE YOU!"

"Sorry, I didn't hear

what you said."

"NEVER MIND!"

Oh, how I wish I had the courage to say I love you to that person...

PERFECTIONISM

CAN DELAY MY

SUCCESS

AND EVEN

PARALYZE ME.

I will be less demanding
of myself.

BE A FRIEND THAT EVERYONE WANTS TO HAVE AROUND.

Be a nice person!

> IF THAT'S THE ONLY
> THING I CAN GET NOW,
> THEN I SHOULD BE
> GRATEFUL FOR IT.

"*OH, WHY DID I TAKE SO LONG TO ACHIEVE MY GOALS?*"

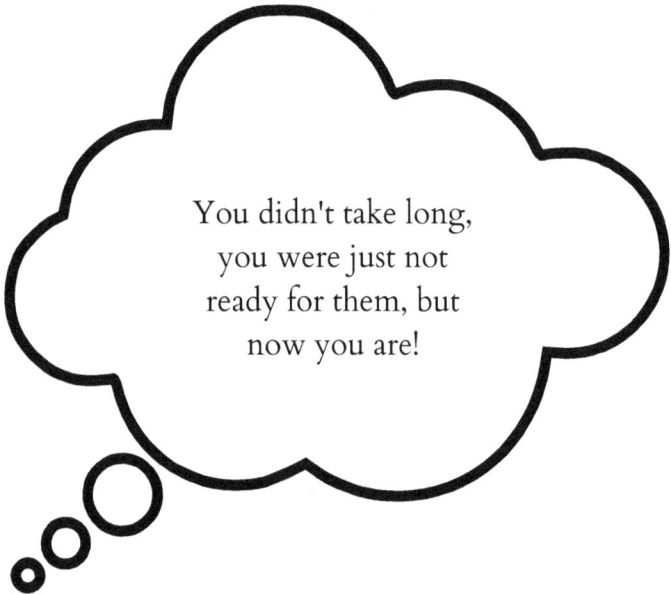

You didn't take long, you were just not ready for them, but now you are!

ADVICE:

APPLY SUNSCREEN

ON YOUR FACE

DAILY!

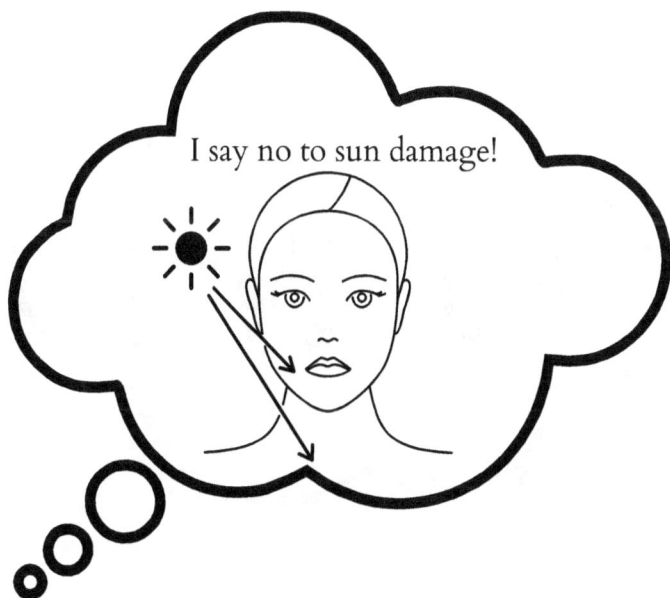

I say no to sun damage!

"HAPPINESS IS...

FAMILY!

"

"

WHAT IS

MEANT

TO BE,

WILL BE!!

"

Please relax and trust!

"

I DON'T UNDERSTAND

WHY MY BODY CAN'T

STAND STILL WHEN I

HEAR THE BEAT

OF GOOD MUSIC.

"

> ## MY BOAT MAY BE SINKING, BUT I'M GOING DOWN SINGING.

Stress won't solve it anyway…

" THINGS WILL HAPPEN

WHEN

THEY SHOULD HAPPEN. "

Don't rush the process!

" YES,

I TALK TO MYSELF.

NO,

I AM NOT CRAZY. "

I am my best
friend and
biggest
supporter!

SPEAKING WISDOM

IS EASY,

MAKING WISE DECISIONS

IS THE HARD PART.

Not everyone will…

"

WE ALL HAVE

TO DEAL

WITH

AWFUL PEOPLE!

"

You are not alone in this!

GOOD MANNERS

WILL NEVER

GO OUT

OF FASHION!

Even though many have
abandoned them, I never will!

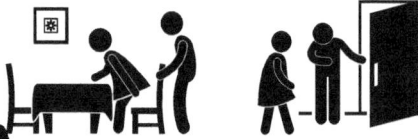

My Comic Quotes

BY MARCIA CHORNEY

> IF YOU WANT TO BE CONSIDERED A TREASURE MORE VALUABLE THAN GOLD AND PRECIOUS STONES, BE A FAITHFUL AND DEDICATED PERSON.

> **ANY RELATIONSHIP**
>
> **IS LIKE A**
>
> # TWO-WAY ROAD;
>
> **CARS COME,**
>
> **AND CARS GO.**

I cannot expect everything to come in just one direction.

"

AFTER A TROPICAL

STORM,

THE SUN

COMES OUT.

"

Remember that...

"

WHEN I AM FEELING

BAD,

I DO

GOOD

FOR SOMEONE.

"

Helping others…
Best medicine for a sad soul!

> I'VE SEEN RICH
>
> LIVING IN POVERTY;
>
> I'VE SEEN POOR
>
> LIVING IN ABUNDANCE.

It was never about money.

" WHEN LIVING

ONE DAY AT A TIME

IS STILL UNBEARABLE

TO YOU, THEN LIVE

ONE MOMENT AT A TIME. "

Manage the now, now;
take a break;
then manage the later, later.

> I WORK LATE INTO THE NIGHT AND WAKE UP BEFORE THE SUN RISE. THAT'S MY RECIPE TO BOOST MY SELF-WORTH.

And it keeps my mind busy!

66

DURING THE SUMMER, I COLLECT THE WOOD FOR THE BONFIRE THAT WILL WARM ME UP DURING THE COLD DAYS OF THE WINTER.

99

I'll take advantage of the good days to prepare for the bad days.

BEING ACCUSED OF

WHAT I DO NOT DO

HURTS AND BLEEDS

AS MUCH AS A REAL

STAB IN THE HEART.

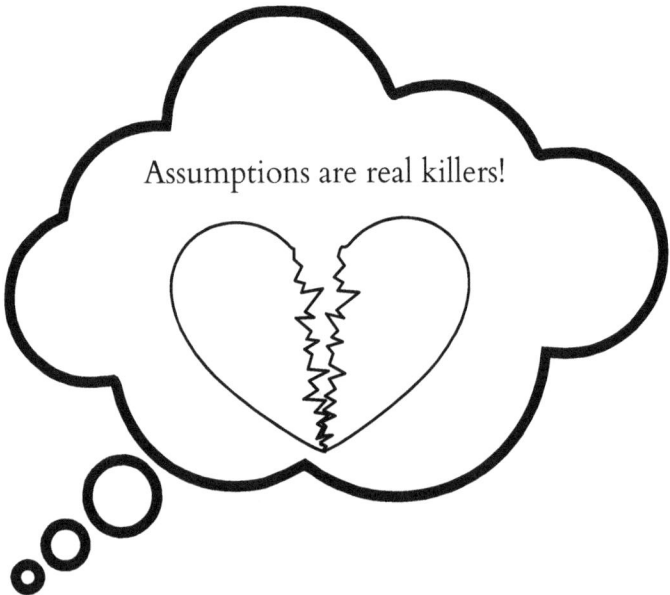

Assumptions are real killers!

WISDOM IS LIKE THE WIND;

IT IS EVERYWHERE BUT IT

CANNOT BE SEEN AND NOT

CAUGHT WITH THE HANDS.

ONLY THOSE WHO FACE

THE WIND WILL BE

INFUSED WITH IT.

Withstand the wind...
the best comes after it.

> TRAGEDIES?
>
> CORRUPTION?
>
> FINANCIAL CRISIS?
>
> BAD NEWS?
>
> LET'S TALK ABOUT LOVE?

Turn off the bad news and talk about good things!

66

A PIECE OF ADVICE

ACCEPTED AND PUT

INTO ACTION

CAN CHANGE

SO MANY THINGS...

99

Ah, if you just accept it...

**I CHALLENGE YOU
TO CHALLENGE THE
NEGATIVE THOUGHTS
THAT COME INTO
YOUR MIND, SPEAKING
THE EXACT OPPOSITE
OF EVERYTHING.**

> # THERE ARE FIGHTS
>
> ## THAT
>
> ## ONLY
>
> # I
>
> ## CAN FIGHT.

HAPPINESS IS...

A CUP OF

HOT CHOCOLATE

ON A COLD DAY.

I am always finding happiness
in the simple things in life.

"

ADVICE FOR THE YOUNG

AT HEART: SOON

YOU WILL BE OLDER,

WHEN ARE YOU GONNA

MAKE IT WORK?*

"

When?

*Tears For Fears

"

IN THE SAME WAY I HAVE

TO EXERCISE MY MUSCLES

IN ORDER TO GET THEM

IN BETTER SHAPE, I HAVE TO

EXERCISE MY MIND

TO CHANGE IT.

"

Think on the logic of this...

"

THE THING

THAT SHOULD

CONCERN ME

THE MOST IS

MY HEALTH.

"

Everything else comes after.

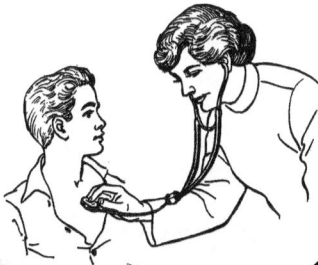

"

FOR THE DAYS

I AM SLOWER

THAN USUAL:

C O F F E E!

"

A much-needed
boost for such days.

"

PICK UP

THE PACE!!

PRESS ON,

FRIEND!!

"

Don't stop!!!

I DON'T LOOK AT THE

SIZE OF THE OBSTACLE.

I LOOK AT THE SIZE

OF MY DESIRE

TO GET THERE!

I can do it!!!

A GOOD

OPPORTUNITY

DOESN'T ALWAYS

COME TWICE.

"

WE DON'T ALWAYS FIT
IN WITH THE FAMILY WE
ARE BORN INTO. BUT WE
DON'T NECESSARILY COME
TO FIT IN, BUT TO
TRANSFORM OURSELVES
AND EACH OTHER.

"

Let your light shine on your family.

FORGIVING

IS

A WAY

TO LOVE.

Others, and yourself.

WHEN I DIDN'T

LISTEN TO

GOOD ADVICE,

I TRIPPED

AND FELL.

I AM 50%

RESPONSIBLE

FOR THE SUCCESS OR

FAILURE OF ALL MY

RELATIONSHIPS.

My actions are important!

"

MY WORDS

ABOUT MYSELF

ARE VITAMIN INJECTIONS

INTO MY VEINS, OR

DEADLY POISONS.

"

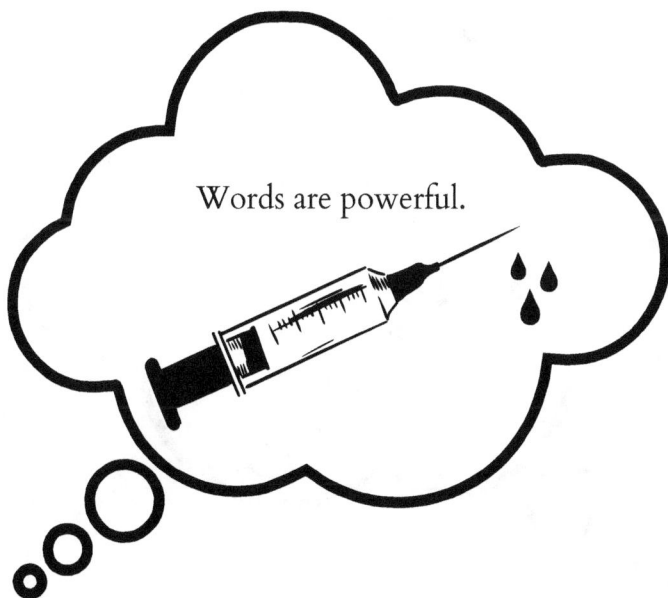

Words are powerful.

> I WANT TO DO ONE THING BUT DON'T HAVE THE BOLDNESS TO DO IT BECAUSE I THINK I'M NOT GOOD ENOUGH. THEN, SOMEONE WHO IS LESS PREPARED THAN ME, DOES IT.

That was my best wake up call!

DREAM

PLAN

ACT

SUCCEED

REJOICE!

Just to dream is not enough.
There are other important steps
before rejoicing.

My Comic Quotes

BY MARCIA CHORNEY

"

WORDS OF

ENCOURAGEMENT

COMING FROM A FRIEND

DURING DIFFICULT TIMES

ARE LIKE

WATER IN THE DESERT.

"

I won't die of
thirst;
I'll call a friend
when I need
encouragement.

" HAPPINESS

IS

SIMPLER

THAN

YOU THINK. "

I won't complicate things.

IT IS HARDER TO BE HAPPY WHILE EATING POORLY AND NOT EXERCISING.

Our mental health is strictly linked to this.

"

BEING UNSTOPPABLE

DOES NOT MEAN THAT

I DON'T HAVE OBSTACLES,

IT MEANS THAT I CRASH

ALL OF THEM IN

ORDER NOT TO STOP.

"

Stopping is not a choice!

WHEN YOU LEARN TO FIGHT WITH YOUR MIND AND MASTER THE STRATEGIES TO OVERCOME IT, YOU GAIN THAT ATTITUDE: BRING IT ON!!!

Such a great feeling of empowerment!

> I DON'T BELIEVE
>
> ALL MY DREAMS.
>
> MANY ARE
>
> # MISLEADING.

I learned it the hard way!

RIGHT

WRONG

MIRROR EXERCISE:

I AM SMART!

I AM STRONG!

I CAN DO IT!

I GOT WHAT IT TAKES!

AND I WILL GET

WHERE I WANT!

It doesn't matter what others think or say!

"

IN A WORLD MADE OF

FAKES,

PRECIOUS ARE THE

ONES MADE OF

TRUTH.

"

May my truth prevail, always!

THERE IS ONLY ONE

"SMALL"

ADVANTAGE TO

SHOWING THE WORLD

YOUR TRUE SELF:

F R E E D O M!

> **I DO GOOD AND TRUST THAT THINGS WILL HAPPEN, NOT IN MY WAY, BUT IN AN EVEN BETTER WAY.**

Faith & Hope!

> I WEAR MY
>
> FAVORITE
>
> PERFUME
>
> JUST FOR MYSELF.

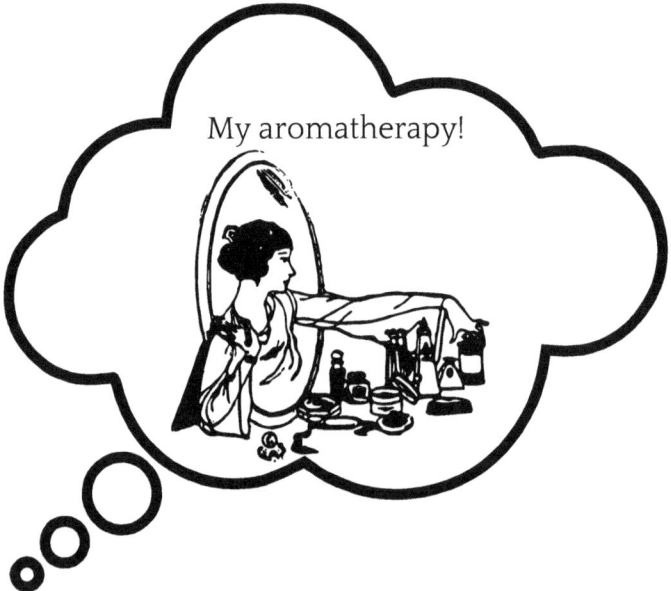

My aromatherapy!

EXCESSIVE

SELF-CRITIQUE

PREVENTS US FROM

ENJOYING A LIGHTER

AND HAPPIER LIFE.

Have more compassion for yourself!

THE VALUE OF A MOMENT IS NOT IN THE TIME IT LASTS, BUT IN THE IMPACT IT HAS ON US OVER TIME.

You will be able to identify what these moments are.

"

I KEEP MY

VALUABLE THINGS

IN A VERY

SAFE PLACE.

"

"YES, OR NO?

WHAT IS THE

RIGHT ANSWER???"

The answer is already
screaming within you...

" HAPPINESS IS A

RATIONAL,

INTENTIONAL AND

UNCONDITIONAL

DECISION. NEVER AN

EMOTIONAL DECISION. "

I won't depend on my emotions to be happy. I'll make a rational decision to be happy today!

> EVERY BATTLE HAS A
>
> # BEGINNING,
>
> # MIDDLE
>
> # AND END.

Hang in there!

"

IF YOU ARE NOT

SATISFIED WITH THE

WORLD YOU LIVE IN, YOU

DON'T HAVE TO LEAVE IT

LITERALLY; CREATE A

BRAND-NEW WORLD

WITHIN YOU!

"

There are no limits
for the human mind!

" SLOW

DOWN! "

Otherwise, you'll miss
the small details.

"

WE MAY LOSE

SOME BATTLES,

BUT WE HAVE WON,

AND WILL WIN

MANY OTHERS.

"

Remember your past victories.

> I HAVE NOT FAILED;
>
> I'VE LEARNED
>
> A VALUABLE
>
> # LESSON.

" RECOGNIZING WHAT'S

NOT POSSIBLE FOR ME

IS ALSO A GOOD LESSON.

LESS UNREALISTIC

EXPECTATIONS,

MORE REALITY! "

As hard as it is...

"

ANY DAY IS

A GOOD DAY

TO REALIGN

MY PRIORITIES.

"

And not to waste more
time on old priorities.

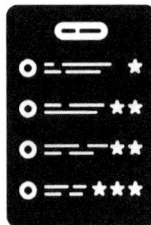

> **WE PLANT ON ONE SIDE**
>
> **AND HARVEST**
>
> **ON THE OTHER.**
>
> **WE PLANT IN ONE WAY,**
>
> **AND HARVEST**
>
> **IN ANOTHER.**

I'll keep planting good seeds
and not worry about the results,
as I know they will come,
and they will be good!

> **I VALUE EVERY SECOND WITH THE PEOPLE I LOVE. ONE DAY THESE MOMENTS WILL NO LONGER EXIST.**

Sad reality.

THAT INCONVENIENT

TRUTH...

"YOU DON'T KNOW

WHAT YOU'VE GOT

UNTIL IS GONE!"*

I'd better realize what
I've got before it's gone!

BYE

*Joni Mitchell

> LIKE A PIECE OF
> BUBBLE GUM WHICH GOES
> INTO THE MOUTH SWEET
> BUT SHORTLY LOSES FLAVOR
> AND IS THROWN AWAY,
> SO IS THE EASY WOMAN.

Value yourself, girl!

HAPPINESS IS...

TO BE TRULY

LOVED

AND CARED FOR!

I won't settle for less than that!

> IF SOMETHING
>
> WITHIN YOU TELLS YOU
>
> THAT THIS MAY BE
>
> YOUR BEST CHANCE
>
> TO BE HAPPY,
>
> # THEN RUN UP TO IT!

The opportunity may not be available for too long. Hurry!!!

"

LET'S NOT BE

DECEIVED...

IT'S NOT EASY

TO FIND PEOPLE

WE CAN TRUST!

"

When I find them,
I'll take good care of them.

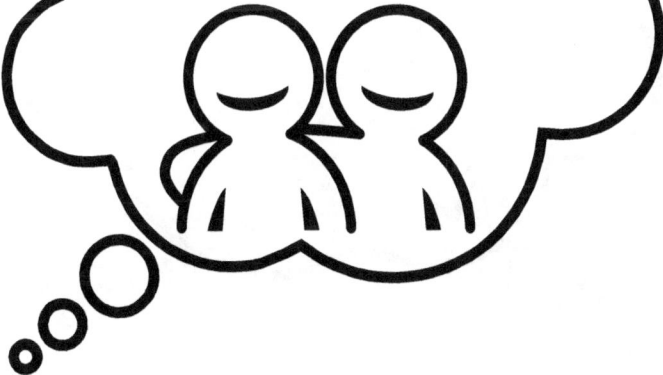

> I FIRMLY BELIEVE
>
> THAT ALL MY EFFORTS
>
> WILL BE REWARDED;
>
> ONE WAY OR ANOTHER.

Therefore,
I'll put a lot of effort into my projects.

My Comic Quotes

BY MARCIA CHORNEY

> ## THERE IS
>
> # A HAPPY, POSITIVE
>
> # AND FUN
>
> ## PERSON THAT IS BEING
>
> ## HELD CAPTIVE
>
> ## INSIDE OF YOU.

TURN THE PAGE!

THAT CHAPTER

IS LONG OVER!

You are already living
the next chapter.

"

BEWARE OF THE TOXIC POSITIVITY MOVEMENT. NO, WE CANNOT BE EVERYTHING WE WANT AND DO EVERYTHING WE WISH.

"

I wish...
but believing in this
is a good recipe for
disappointment.

> I WANT TO BECOME
>
> AN INTERESTING
>
> PERSON, FULL OF
>
> STORIES TO TELL.

And for that to happen,
I must live intensely!

" IT WILL BE HARD

TO WALK FORWARD

WITH THESE CHAINS

PULLING YOU BACK. "

Get rid of them first,

and then move forward.

"*That will never*

happen to me."

BELIEVING IN THIS

IS THE FIRST STEP...

Thinking that something bad is going to happen attracts a dark cloud of negativity around you.

"IF SOMETHING BOTHERS ME,

I REPLACE IT. AFTER THAT,

IF IT BOTHERS ME AGAIN,

I REPLACE IT AGAIN. IT BOTHERS

ME ONE MORE TIME,

I KEEP ON CHANGING IT...

THINGS, PLACES AND PEOPLE,

UNTIL I FIND MY PEACE.

But isn't this the time to think about whether the problem is with me?

"NEED"

IS THE BEST

HUMAN MOTIVATOR.

IF YOU'RE IN IT,

TAKE ADVANTAGE AND

USE IT IN YOUR FAVOR.

Take this motivating wave
to get you moving!

TODAY I MAY BE

LOOKING IN FROM

OUTSIDE THE FENCE.

BUT ONE DAY

I WILL BE INSIDE.

It's all up to me!

> ## ALTHOUGH I AM A
> # LITTLE TINY PART
> ## OF THIS WORLD, I AM
> ## A VERY IMPORTANT
> ## PART OF IT!

I was put into it for a purpose,
and not by chance.

" WHILE IT IS NOT READY

IT WILL NOT ARRIVE.

THINGS TAKE THEIR

OWN TIME TO GET

INTO OUR LIVES. "

I need to learn to wait patiently.

I TRUST THE SEA WAVES OF LIFE, ALWAYS TAKING THE BAD THINGS AWAY FROM ME, AND BRINGING THE GOOD THINGS CLOSE TO ME.

I sit on the beach of life contemplating this beautiful movement...

ADOLESCENCE:

ONE OF THE

BEST PHASES

OF OUR LIVES.

If you're in it,
don't let your mind
sabotage this wonderful time.

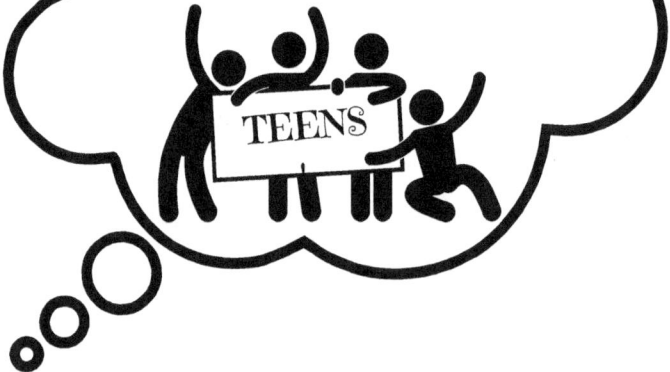

TEENS

"

BEING DIFFERENT

FROM THE OTHERS

IS NOT A DEFECT,

IT'S A QUALITY.

"

The world is more beautiful
with this diversity.

"

A

LOOK

SAYS

IT

ALL!

"

It's the simplest expression of everything that's inside, but we don't have the courage to say it.

"

THERE ARE PEOPLE

WHO DON'T WANT

TO DO

ANYTHING

BUT WANT TO WIN

EVERYTHING.

"

It's not going to happen!
The sowing and reaping law
never fails. It won't be reaped
if it hasn't been planted.

WHEN I'M NOT

CATCHING FISH

FROM ONE SIDE,

I THROW MY NET

TO THE OTHER SIDE.

I'll change my strategy!

" WHOEVER HAS NOT MADE MISTAKES IN LIFE IS NOT THAT INTERESTING. THEY DON'T HAVE A LOT OF STORIES TO TELL. "

Making mistakes also has its advantages!

> # REALITY CHECK:
>
> ## AT THE END OF
>
> ## OUR MOVIE,
>
> ## THE MAIN
>
> ## CHARACTER DIES.

What do I really want to do while I'm still acting on it?

> WE DO NOT HAVE
>
> THE POWER
>
> TO CHANGE
>
> ANYONE BUT
>
> OURSELVES.

Give up and
don't insist on it.

" HAPPINESS IS...

PICNIC ON THE BEACH

AT THE SUNSET. "

Moments that remind us
that life is worth living!

"

I DO NOT WAIT TO ACT ONLY AFTER RECEIVING INFORMATION FROM OTHERS. I SEARCH MYSELF FOR THE INFORMATION I NEED.

"

I run after the things I want!

> IT IS CERTAIN THAT
> NOT ALL TALENTED PEOPLE
> IN THE WORLD WILL HAVE
> A PLACE IN THE SPOTLIGHT.
> HOWEVER, ALL SACRIFICE
> PRODUCES GOOD RESULTS.

I will strive in everything I do!

EVERYTHING

CHANGES.

INCLUDING

OURSELVES.

And I'm glad that we change...

" WHEN I TURNED AWAY

FROM THE THINGS THAT

WERE HOLDING ME BACK,

EVERYTHING STARTED

TO QUICKLY

MOVE FORWARD. "

Free yourself from those
who hold you back!

> DON'T SHARE YOUR PROBLEMS
>
> ON SOCIAL MEDIA. PEOPLE
>
> DON'T CARE, THEY JUST PUSH
>
> # THE "LIKE" BUTTON,
>
> WHICH IS A VERY
>
> DIFFERENT THING.

Don't get things wrong and share with those who actually care about you.

"

"That person left my life unexpectedly, and I haven't done anything wrong to deserve it!" **DON'T WORRY, IT'S THE NECESSARY CLEANING THAT HAPPENS IN OUR LIVES FROM TIME TO TIME.**

"

Those who should not participate in our victories with us must leave before them.

BYE

WE ARE PREDESTINED TO BE HAPPY, BUT THEN WHEN WE GET HERE, WE FIND ALL THE REASONS NOT TO BE.

I think it's time to simplify things...

"

I WONDER HOW THE WORLD

WOULD BE IF ALL THE

CREATIVE GENIUSES HAD

NOT HAD THE COURAGE

TO FIGHT FOR THEIR

DREAMS AND PROJECTS.

"

It sure wouldn't be an interesting place.

$E=MC^2$

> **I ENJOY MY AGE. I AM NOT SORRY FOR THE YEARS PASSED, AND FOR THE YOUTH THAT'S GOING AWAY EACH YEAR. EACH STAGE OF LIFE HAS ITS BEAUTY.**

They were very well lived years!

My Comic
Quotes

BY MARCIA CHORNEY

> **YOU WILL ONLY START BEARING FRUIT WHEN YOUR INNER DESIRE IS SO GREAT THAT IT WILL CAUSE AN INTERNAL EXPLOSION.**

That will destroy
all your inner barriers,
and also, your excuses...

"WHEN I STOPPED DREAMING, THINGS STOPPED HAPPENING. WHEN I STARTED DREAMING AGAIN, THINGS STARTED TO HAPPEN AGAIN."

From now on,
I will never stop dreaming!

" IT'S IN A TIME OF ARGUMENT THAT PEOPLE LET OUT WHAT THEY REALLY THINK OF ME. "

It's my opportunity to find out if I should stay close to that person, or if I should stay away.

> # A NOTE FROM
>
> # MY FUTURE SELF
>
> # TO
>
> # MY PRESENT SELF:
>
> # B E H A P P Y!

Life is really fleeting...

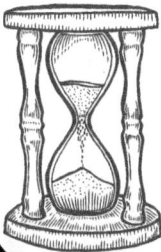

THERE ARE THINGS IN LIFE THAT ARE LIKE WALKING IN THE DARK. I MUST HAVE COURAGE, AND EVEN WITHOUT SEEING ANYTHING,

I MUST BELIEVE!

I just need to remember that it is not wise to run in the dark; So, I'll take it one step at a time.

" THERE'S SOMETHING

MAGIC

IN WRITING

WHAT I WANT

TO ACHIEVE. "

I will meditate on them;
I will work for them!

I KEEP MY DREAMS

SECRET.

NOT EVERYONE WILL

WISH THEM

TO COME TRUE.

> **THOSE WHO NEVER RECOGNIZE MY VALUE WILL CONTINUE NOT RECOGNIZING EVEN IF I CONQUERED THE WORLD.**

I will win for me and
for the people who cheer for me,
and not for them.

"

LIVE AT THE TOP

OF THE WORLD!

CHANGE YOUR BAD

WAY OF THINKING.

"

The sky is the limit...

"

I NEED

A LITTLE

LOVE

POTION!

"

Or maybe a lot?
Especially the one that removes the
blindfold from my eyes and makes me
see the frog as a frog and not as
a prince or princess.

I CAN CHANGE ANY SITUATION AND CIRCUMSTANCE OF MY LIFE, BECAUSE NOTHING IS CHANGELESS, BUT CHANGEABLE.

Absolutely! Nothing is lost...

66

YOU HAVE

NO EXCUSE

WHEN

JUDGING

OTHERS.

99

" "

THOSE IN A HURRY

EAT RAW,

AS PER THE

POPULAR SAYING...

" "

I've eaten it raw so many times because I didn't know how to wait... It tasted really bad...

> # THOSE WHO SEEK
>
> # WISDOM
>
> ## VALUE THEIR LIFE.

The key to a peaceful life.

THERE IS AN

EXTRAORDINARY

PERSON INSIDE OF YOU,

BUT IT DOESN'T

ALWAYS COME OUT.

What is holding you back?

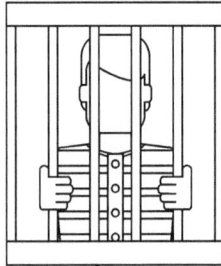

"

A PROBLEM

SOMETIMES CREATES

SPACE FOR

FANTASTIC IDEAS.

"

When the wall appeared
in front of me, an idea on
how to climb it came up.

> **YOU WILL ONLY BE ABLE TO TRULY IDENTIFY THE WRONG ONES WHEN THE RIGHT ONE ARRIVES.**

The difference is obvious, and it's best not to dwell on the wrong ones, not to miss the chance to see the right one.

66

LIFE WILL CAUSE

SITUATIONS TO ANSWER

THE QUESTIONS YOU SO

WANT TO HAVE

THE ANSWERS FOR.

99

Pay attention and accept
the answers...

YES!

NO!

I NEVER STOP STUDYING. I FINISH ONE COURSE AND START ANOTHER.

I keep my brain active!

> **NO ONE IS JUSTIFIED**
>
> **TO MAKE**
>
> # 1000 MISTAKES
>
> **WITH OTHERS, JUST**
>
> **BECAUSE SOMEONE MADE**
>
> **1 MISTAKE WITH THEM.**

I'll be fair and kind to those who never hurt me.

> # WHEN YOU SAY THAT SOMEONE IS A BAD PERSON, YOU ARE SHOWING WHO THE BAD PERSON TRULY IS.

Your actions speak louder than your words.

"
I DON'T CONSUME MY

MIND AND MY HEART

REPENTING FOR LOST TIME.

I THINK: "I WAS NOT READY

THERE, AS I AM READY HERE."
"

That same old story:
there is a right time for everything.

"

THOSE WHO USE THEIR

UNDERSTANDING AND

WISDOM WELL, THRIVE

IN EVERYTHING THEY DO.

"

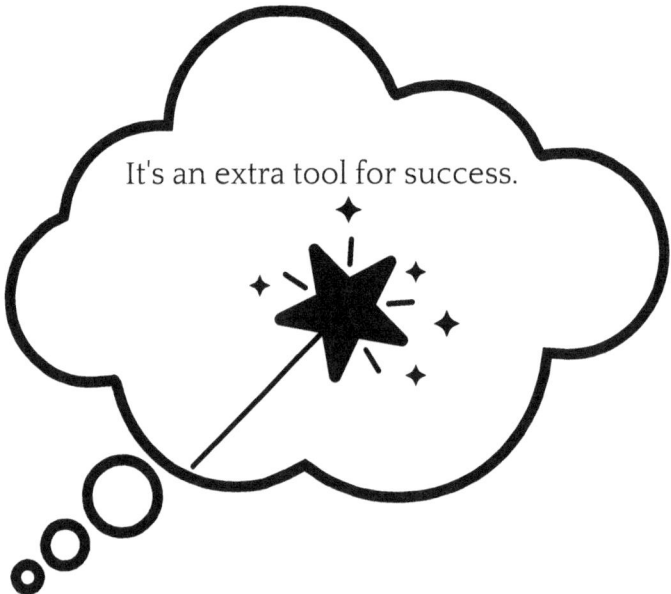

It's an extra tool for success.

> # BEING
>
> # MISINTERPRETED
>
> ## IS A
>
> ## BIG PROBLEM.

> **IF YOU KEEP INSISTING THAT A PERSON, WHO DOES NOT VALUE YOU, STAYS IN YOUR LIFE, YOU WILL BE MISSING TIME AND OPPORTUNITY WITH THE PEOPLE WHO REALLY SEE VALUE IN YOU.**

Let them go!!
It hurts, but it will open the door
for others to approach you.

"

I LIKE TO BE A LITTLE

MYSTERIOUS

& DISCREET.

I DON'T TELL EVERYTHING

OF MY LIFE TO EVERYONE.

"

I like to leave some stories
untold for the proper occasion.

THERE ARE PEOPLE WHO HAVE NO OTHER EXPLANATION... THEY ARE THE STONE IN MY SHOE!!

They came to this world with a single mission: To push all my buttons!!

> TO PROPERLY RESPECT AND LOVE
> A PERSON, I MUST UNDERSTAND
> THEIR PERSPECTIVES AND POINTS
> OF VIEW. THIS WILL BE THE
> EASIEST AND MOST NATURAL WAY
> TO FIX MY ACTIONS
> TOWARDS THAT PERSON.

Respect comes naturally
after this.

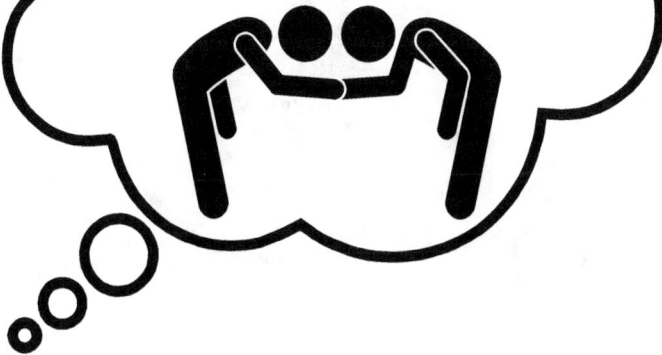

> # I AM A PERSON WHO ALWAYS HAS SOMETHING HAPPENING.

I look for things to get excited about.

A LITTLE BIT

OF PRIDE

IS GOOD

SOMETIMES.

It becomes a self-protection
mechanism.

> IF I DON'T HAVE A DOG,
>
> I'LL HUNT WITH A CAT,
>
> AS THE POPULAR
>
> SAYING GOES,
>
> BUT I WON'T STOP
>
> LOOKING FOR WHAT I WANT.

About the Author

Marcia, a lawyer, mediator and coach, has been deeply passionate about emotional intelligence and psychology from a young age. She embarked on an investigative journey into the realm of emotions, always the observant child in her family, questioning everyone about everything. Indeed, she was the child incessantly asking "why" at every opportunity. Her fascination grew towards analyzing human behavior in relation to emotions. Through personal experiences, she realized the profound impact emotions have on our life's path and decision-making processes.

After exploring this vast sea of emotions and gaining insights, she turned to writing to guide others in understanding and appreciating this complex world, which is often avoided by many and seen as a dangerous place to navigate. The author believes that the quicker we comprehend our emotions, the sooner we can master them, turning the daunting, mysterious ocean of emotions into a serene, navigable lake with clear, shallow waters.

For more information about the author and her forthcoming books, please visit www.marciachorney.com

Acknowledgments

Many people encourage our dreams directly or indirectly, continuously, throughout our lives, or briefly; so, it would be impossible to mention here all the people who have passed through my life and lit a flame in me, besides those who currently encouraged me, in one way or another, to make this dream come true.

First, I want to thank God for my life, and for putting so much love in my heart for those who are going through emotional challenges. It is this love that motivates me to write.

Thanks to my family, who are my refuge and my support base, and without them, it would be harder to achieve my life goals. Special thanks to Isabella and Mikaella.

To the dear Wilson family for their love and support throughout this project.

To all my friends who are not mentioned here but who always encourage me to fight for my dreams, in addition to those who, even unknowingly, awakened in me some of my old dreams that were asleep.

A big and warm thanks from the bottom of my heart!

(Marcia Chorney)

Emotional Intelligence Collection